P9-COO-302

I Love

Wild Cats

By Steve Parker
Illustrated by Ian Jackson

SANDY CREEK

© 2007 by Miles Kelly Publishing Ltd

This 2008 edition published by Sandy Creek
by arrangement with Miles Kelly Publishing Ltd.

Editorial Director Belinda Gallagher
Art Director Jo Brewer
Creative Artworker Rick Caylor
Assistant Editor Lucy Dowling
Cover Artworker Stephan Davis
Production Manager Elizabeth Brunwin
Reprographics Stephan Davis, Ian Paulyn

Sandy Creek
122 Fifth Avenue
New York, NY 10011

ISBN-13: 978-0-7607-9057-1
ISBN-10: 0-7607-9057-4

Library of Congress Cataloging-in-Publication-Data
on file at the Library of Congress

Printed and bound in Thailand

3 5 7 9 10 8 6 4 2

www.mileskelly.net
info@mileskelly.net

Contents

Snow leopard

The snow leopard lives in the high mountains of Central Asia. It prefers to live on its own and is very difficult to spot in the wild. Unlike most big cats, the snow leopard cannot roar.

A long, thick fur coat helps to keep the snow leopard warm in the cold mountains.

Smallest cat

The smallest big cat is the clouded leopard of Southeast Asia. It likes to live in the trees.

4

This rare big cat hunts in mountain forests for goats, sheep, birds, and monkeys.

The snow leopard has sharp claws. It keeps them sharp and clean by pulling them up inside the pads on its paws.

Cheetah

The cheetah is the fastest animal on land. This big cat races along almost as fast as a car on a freeway. The cheetah can only keep this speed up for half a minute. Then it must stop to cool down and get its breath back.

Dry, open areas such as grasslands are the best places for cheetahs to hunt. They couldn't run very fast in a thick wood!

The cheetah has very long legs, a slim and bendy body, and a small head.

Cheetahs hunt small gazelles, antelopes, hares, and other fast-running animals.

Claws out!
Unlike other big cats, the cheetah cannot pull its claws into its toes. The claws are big and blunt, like a dog's.

The cheetah tries to knock over its victim, before pouncing on it.

7

Leopard

Sometimes a leopard catches prey that is too big to eat in one meal. The leopard stores the leftovers in a tree, where it is kept safe from hungry hyenas and jackals.

Every leopard has a different pattern of spots—just like every person has different fingerprints.

Black leopard!

The black panther is not a different kind of big cat. It's a leopard with dark fur.

The leopard's favorite tree has scratch marks in the bark to warn other leopards to keep away.

8

A leopard can catch large animals such as antelopes. When food is scarce, it will eat anything, even beetles!

The leopard is strong enough to drag a whole gazelle up into a tree.

Siberian tiger

The Siberian tiger is the biggest cat.
This huge hunter prowls the cold, snowy
lands of eastern Asia. It is the rarest kind
of tiger, with less than 200 left in the wild.

Thick fur keeps
the tiger warm in
the ice and snow.

The tiger has
long fur on its
cheeks, making its
face look wide.

Tigers have orange fur with black stripes. The Siberian tiger has more white in its coat to help it blend in with its snowy landscape.

Maneaters!

Tigers that attack people are usually old or injured. They can't catch their normal prey such as deer or wild cattle.

The Siberian tiger is heavily built. Its body hangs close to the ground.

Lion

Lions are the only big cats that live in a group. A group of lions is called a pride. There are usually between five and ten lions in a pride. They are mostly mothers with their young, and one or two males.

In a pride, the chief male lion is the father of all the cubs. His main job is to chase away other lions so that they cannot steal food.

Male and female lions look different. The male is bigger and has long, shaggy neck fur called a mane.

Lions roar loudly to frighten off other lions that aren't in their pride.

Padded paws

Lions have thick, leathery pads on the underside of their paws. These help the lion to grip tightly and to move quietly.

Puma

Like all big cats, the female puma is a very caring mother. She protects her babies, feeds them on her milk, and keeps them warm and safe in a den. A mother puma usually has two or three cubs, but there may be as many as six!

Puma cubs feed on their mother's milk for seven weeks. Then they begin to eat meat brought to them by their mother.

Useful tails

Like the puma, the domestic cat has a long tail. This helps it to balance as it walks along narrow surfaces.

The mother puma licks her babies clean. She often moves them to a new den for extra safety.

The cubs have spotty coats when they are first born. The spots fade as the cubs get older.

Caracal

All cats can jump well, but one of the best leapers is the caracal. This cat is not very big, but it could jump over a car in one leap. It can even jump straight upwards, leaping as high as the ceiling from standing still!

The caracal lives in dry places such as rocky hills, grasslands, and around the edges of deserts.

Champion leap!

The caracal can jump four times its own body length. See how far you can jump!

This cat crouches down and then springs forwards using its powerful rear legs.

Long tufts
of fur on the
caracal's ears make
it look like another
big cat—the lynx.

A light-brown coat
helps the caracal to
hide in long grass
or sandy deserts.

Serval

All cats have amazing senses to help them hunt for food. The serval has large eyes to help it see in the dark. Its long, stiff whiskers help it to feel its way. Its big ears pick up tiny sounds and its nose sniffs for food and danger.

When the serval pounces it holds down its prey with its claws. Long, sharp teeth help the serval to kill and eat its meal.

The serval's favorite meals include swamp rats, water voles, and baby ducks.

The serval's spotty coat helps it to hide from its prey in the long grass.

Cat's eyes!
Cat's eyes have a shiny lining inside them. Light bounces off this lining and makes the eyes glow in the dark.

Using its long, slim legs, the serval leaps quickly from its hiding place.

19

Lynx

The lynx lives in the snow and ice of the far north. It has very thick fur to keep it warm. Its paws are large and wide, and they have fur underneath, too. The paws work like snowshoes, to prevent the lynx sinking into soft snow, or sliding on slippery ice.

After hunting, the lynx may bury spare food in the snow and come back to eat it later.

Snow paws!

Press your fingers into some flour. Now put a bag over your hand. See how your "snow paw" sinks in less.

The lynx has a very short tail. A long tail would get too cold in the freezing winter.

The furry tufts on the tips of the lynx's ears keep its ears warm in the icy air.

Wide, furry paws help the lynx to grip on snow, ice, wet rocks, and slippery tree branches.

21

Jaguar

The jaguar is a good swimmer and it likes to hunt around rivers, lakes, and swamps. It catches water creatures such as turtles, deer, crayfish, and snakes. It even dives under the surface to chase fish!

After a swim, the jaguar cleans and combs its fur, using its rough tongue and its sharp claws.

The jaguar creeps slowly through water without a splash or a ripple to surprise its prey.

A spotted coat helps the jaguar to blend in with leaves and twigs around it.

American cat

The jaguar is South America's biggest cat. With its spotty coat, it is similar to the leopard of Africa and Asia.

Fun facts

Snow leopard The female snow leopard keeps warm by lining her den with her own fur.

Cheetah In the wild, cheetahs only live for about 10 to 12 years because the older they get, the slower they become.

Siberian tiger When they want to be friendly, Siberian tigers blow through their nostrils and playfully bite each other's necks.

Caracal The caracal can kill an antelope more than twice its own weight.

Serval These long-legged leapers make a purring sound like a pet cat.

Leopard The jaws of a leopard are so strong, it can lift prey the same size as itself.

Lynx The lynx changes the color of its coat according to the seasons. In winter its coat is light gray in color and in the summer it is light brown.

Jaguar These big cats can be found living on grassland but they prefer to live in cool, thick forests.

Puma The puma cannot roar, instead it makes an ear-piercing scream.

Lion Male lions start to grow a mane at three years of age.